All About the
PERIODIC
TABLE

Georgia Beth

Consultants

Benjamin Andrews
Geologist and Associate Curator of
Rocks and Ores
National Museum of Natural History

Cheryl Lane, M.Ed.
Seventh Grade Science Teacher
Chino Valley Unified School District

Michelle Wertman, M.S.Ed.
Literacy Specialist
New York City Public Schools

Publishing Credits

Rachelle Cracchiolo, M.S.Ed., *Publisher*
Emily R. Smith, M.A.Ed., *SVP of Content Development*
Véronique Bos, *VP of Creative*
Dani Neiley, *Editor*
Robin Erickson, *Senior Art Director*

Smithsonian Enterprises

Avery Naughton, *Licensing Coordinator*
Paige Towler, *Editorial Lead*
Jill Corcoran, *Senior Director, Licensed Publishing*
Brigid Ferraro, *Vice President of New Business and Licensing*
Carol LeBlanc, *President*

Image Credits: p. 9 NASA; p. 10 (top) Bridgeman Images; p. 11 (top) Getty Images;
p. 12 (top) Getty Images; p. 13 Library of Congress [92517587]; p. 15 (top) Courtesy
Edward Tufte, (bottom) Library of Congress [HEC 34087]; p. 16 (top) Bo Arrhed/Alamy;
p. 17 (top) NASA; p. 25 (bottom) Alamy; all other images from iStock and/or Shutterstock or
in the public domain

✺ Smithsonian

5482 Argosy Avenue
Huntington Beach, CA 92649
www.tcmpub.com
ISBN 979-8-7659-6873-4
© 2024 Teacher Created Materials, Inc.
Printed by: 51497
Printed in: China

Table of Contents

The Basic Ingredients

It's lunchtime, and you're hungry. You want something spicy and comforting. By combining a little of this and a little of that, you've made a delicious curry. If you had different ingredients, you might have made a sandwich or a burrito. It all depends on the foods you have and what you're hungry for!

Just like your lunch, everything in the world is made up of ingredients. **Elements** are the building blocks of everything in the universe. Hydrogen and oxygen combine to make water. Sodium and chlorine combine to make salt.

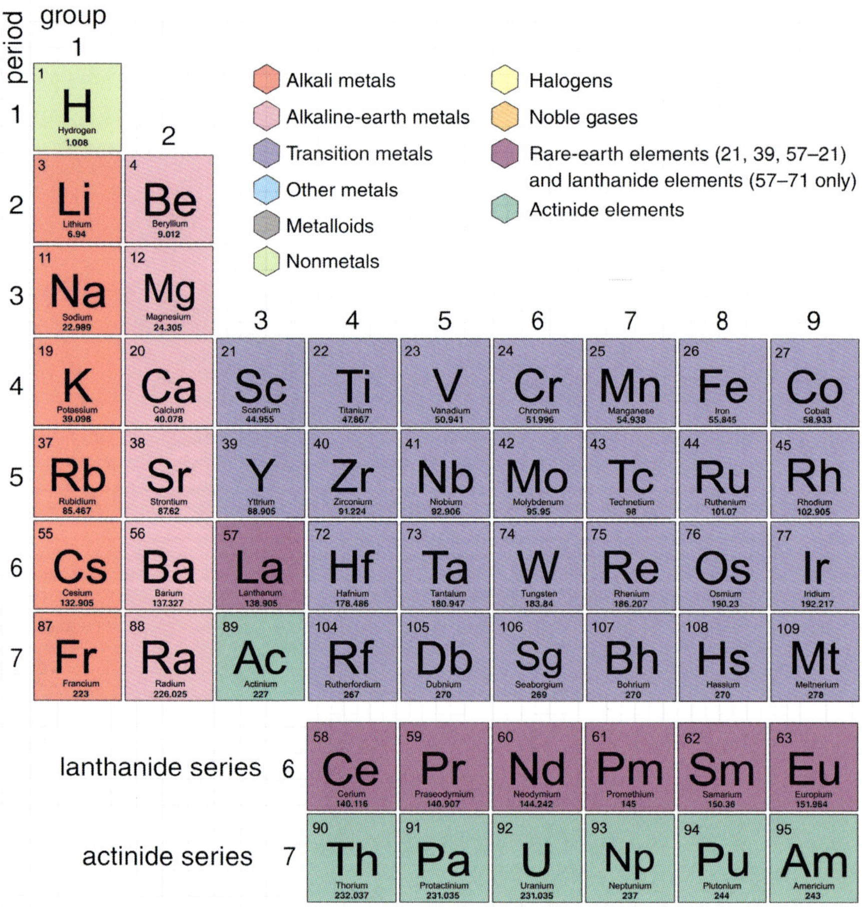

Legend	
Alkali metals	Halogens
Alkaline-earth metals	Noble gases
Transition metals	Rare-earth elements (21, 39, 57–21) and lanthanide elements (57–71 only)
Other metals	Actinide elements
Metalloids	
Nonmetals	

period / group

group	1	2	3	4	5	6	7	8	9
period 1	1 **H** Hydrogen 1.008								
2	3 **Li** Lithium 6.94	4 **Be** Beryllium 9.012							
3	11 **Na** Sodium 22.989	12 **Mg** Magnesium 24.305							
4	19 **K** Potassium 39.098	20 **Ca** Calcium 40.078	21 **Sc** Scandium 44.955	22 **Ti** Titanium 47.867	23 **V** Vanadium 50.941	24 **Cr** Chromium 51.996	25 **Mn** Manganese 54.938	26 **Fe** Iron 55.845	27 **Co** Cobalt 58.933
5	37 **Rb** Rubidium 85.467	38 **Sr** Strontium 87.62	39 **Y** Yttrium 88.905	40 **Zr** Zirconium 91.224	41 **Nb** Niobium 92.906	42 **Mo** Molybdenum 95.95	43 **Tc** Technetium 98	44 **Ru** Ruthenium 101.07	45 **Rh** Rhodium 102.905
6	55 **Cs** Cesium 132.905	56 **Ba** Barium 137.327	57 **La** Lanthanum 138.905	72 **Hf** Hafnium 178.486	73 **Ta** Tantalum 180.947	74 **W** Tungsten 183.84	75 **Re** Rhenium 186.207	76 **Os** Osmium 190.23	77 **Ir** Iridium 192.217
7	87 **Fr** Francium 223	88 **Ra** Radium 226.025	89 **Ac** Actinium 227	104 **Rf** Rutherfordium 267	105 **Db** Dubnium 270	106 **Sg** Seaborgium 269	107 **Bh** Bohrium 270	108 **Hs** Hassium 270	109 **Mt** Meitnerium 278

lanthanide series 6	58 **Ce** Cerium 140.116	59 **Pr** Praseodymium 140.907	60 **Nd** Neodymium 144.242	61 **Pm** Promethium 145	62 **Sm** Samarium 150.36	63 **Eu** Europium 151.964
actinide series 7	90 **Th** Thorium 232.037	91 **Pa** Protactinium 231.035	92 **U** Uranium 231.035	93 **Np** Neptunium 237	94 **Pu** Plutonium 244	95 **Am** Americium 243

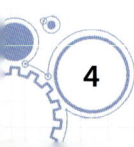

Hydrogen and helium are a bit like bread and butter—they are commonly found. Elements such as chromium and titanium are rarer. Everything from rocks to tomatoes exists because different elements combined in different ways.

The periodic table of elements is a list of all the discovered elements in the universe. Every element is described in basic terms. And similar elements are grouped by the **properties** they share. The periodic table organizes all this information in one easy-to-read chart. It is a useful tool in the **chemistry** field. Today, the periodic table is used daily by scientists and students around the world.

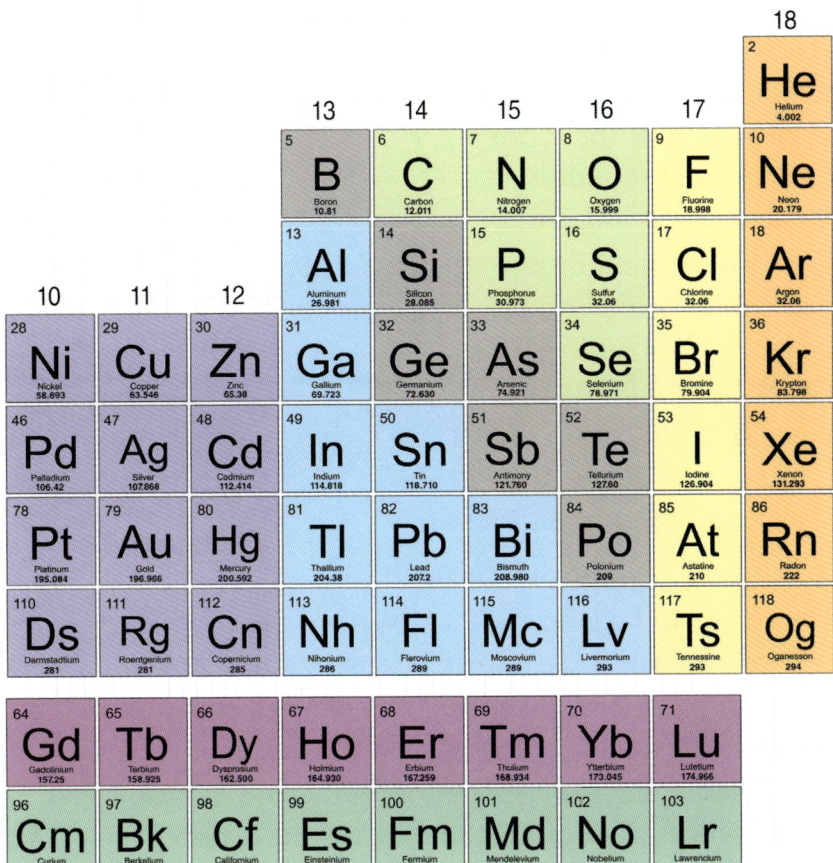

A Brief History of Atoms

Before diving into the information presented in the periodic table, we have to go back in time—and start small. Throughout history, people have wondered what objects on Earth are made of. They have questioned how objects break down, too. For example, what would happen if you sliced an object into tinier and tinier parts? We know that smashing a rock can break it into smaller pieces. But how can a tomato be divided into pieces when, at some point in cutting it smaller and smaller, it turns into red mush? And are tomatoes and rocks made of the same things deep down, even though they look and behave differently?

In ancient Greece, philosophers had many theories about the world. They argued that the world is composed of tiny things that can't be cut into more pieces. They called those units **atoms**. The word *atom* means "indivisible" in Greek. Democritus, a philosopher, had a hypothesis. He argued that everything on Earth is composed of particles.

Democritus

Eventually, scientists were able to test his idea. In fact, scientists advanced the theories of many early thinkers. Scientists discovered that atoms make up everything in the universe. They learned that atoms are smaller than cells, and they can only be seen by the most powerful electron microscopes. Scientists have been studying atoms in-depth for more than 200 years!

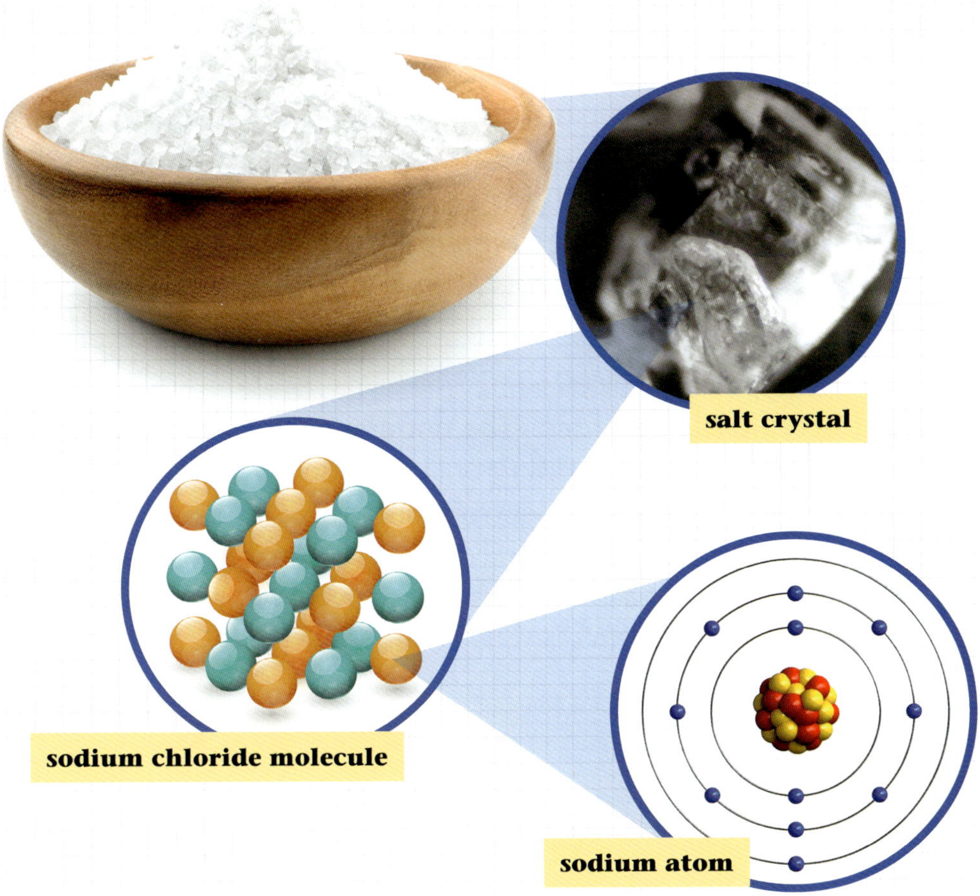

salt crystal
sodium chloride molecule
sodium atom

FUN FACT

Democritus proposed many theories during his life. He was the first person in recorded history to attempt to explain how colors work. He thought colors were caused by the position of atoms. In his theory, black was caused by bumpy and uneven atoms. White was caused by even and smooth atoms. Today, scientists know that colors are different wavelengths of light.

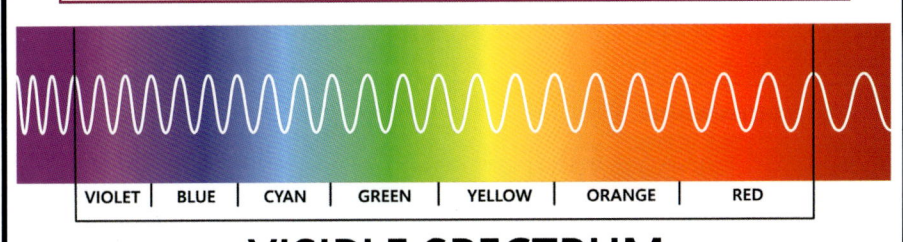

VIOLET
BLUE
CYAN
GREEN
YELLOW
ORANGE
RED

VISIBLE SPECTRUM

Subatomic Particles

Modern scientists learned that atoms can be divided into smaller particles. These are **subatomic** particles. There are three types. The first and second types are **protons** and **neutrons**. They are found in the nucleus of an atom. **Electrons** are the third type. These move around protons and neutrons.

Each type of particle is different. First, protons are heavy and have positive charges. The number of protons is an atom's defining trait. Adding or subtracting protons changes the way atoms behave. Neutrons are similar in size and mass to protons but don't have any charge. Electrons are tiny and lightweight. Each one has a negative charge equal in strength to the proton's positive charge.

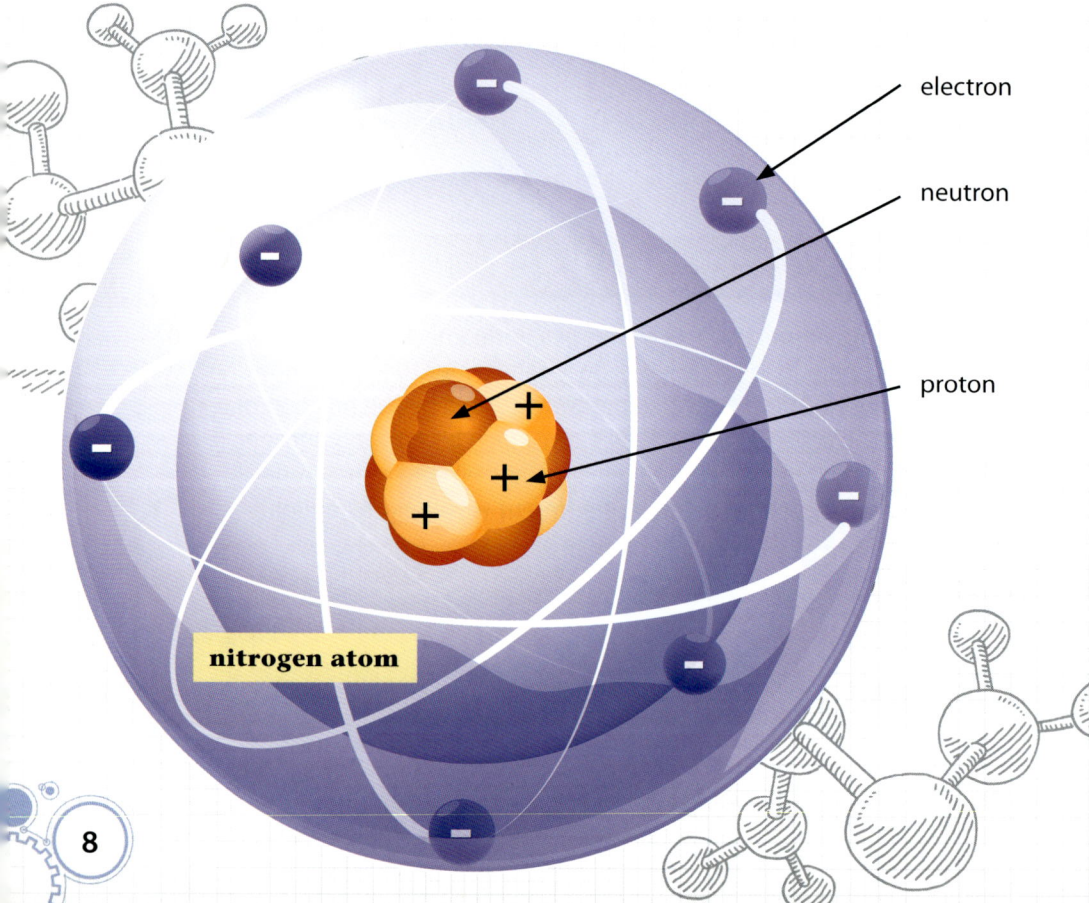

electron

neutron

proton

nitrogen atom

Making Molecules

Atoms combine in different ways to form new molecules. Some molecules are made of two atoms. Others are made of thousands.

Through chemical reactions, atoms combine into new molecules. When this happens, no atoms are created or destroyed. Molecules that combine are called *reactants*. The bonds between atoms break, and new bonds form. The new molecules are called *products*.

Each different type of atom is a unique element. Some atoms can form molecules by themselves. Atoms of different elements can combine to form more complex molecules.

Combining vinegar with baking soda causes a chemical reaction.

Orion Nebula

TECHNOLOGY

New Compounds

Some chemists use elements to develop new **compounds**. In the last 200 years, they have discovered nearly 15 million compounds! Some of these compounds can also be found organically. In June 2023, astronomers using the James Webb Space Telescope detected a compound for the first time. It is called *methyl cation* (MEH-thul CAT-eye-on). It was found in a nebula about 1,350 light years away from Earth!

The Origins of the Periodic Table

For many years, scientists struggled to understand elements. It was also unclear how elements could be combined. And no one knew what rules applied. Scientists wanted to describe and organize elements in ways that would help people understand their interactions.

In the early 1800s, a chemist named John Dalton took steps to solve this. He combined two ideas. The first idea was known as Proust's Law. It said that the components of a chemical compound always combine in the same proportions. For example, two hydrogen atoms and one oxygen atom make one molecule of water. So, you will always need twice as many hydrogen atoms as oxygen atoms. That's true whether you make one molecule or one million molecules of water. The second idea came from ancient Greek thinkers. They had the idea that the atom is the basic unit of matter. Dalton combined these two ideas to build the atomic theory of matter. This let scientists describe everything in the universe in terms of atoms.

John Dalton

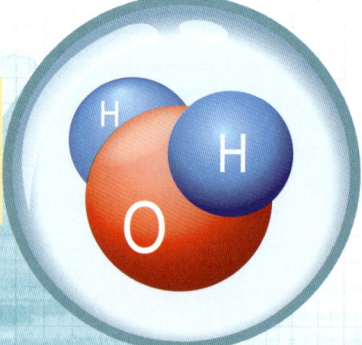

In any amount of water, there are always twice as many hydrogen atoms as there are oxygen atoms.

A First Attempt

In 1862, a French scientist found that atoms can be grouped by the ways they act. He saw there were recurring patterns. He organized the elements by plotting them on a spiral graph. Then, the graph was arranged on a vertical cylinder. Known as the Telluric Screw, it revealed interesting patterns in the elements. But it was hard to visualize, print, and share. Few scientists paid attention to this idea.

Telluric Screw

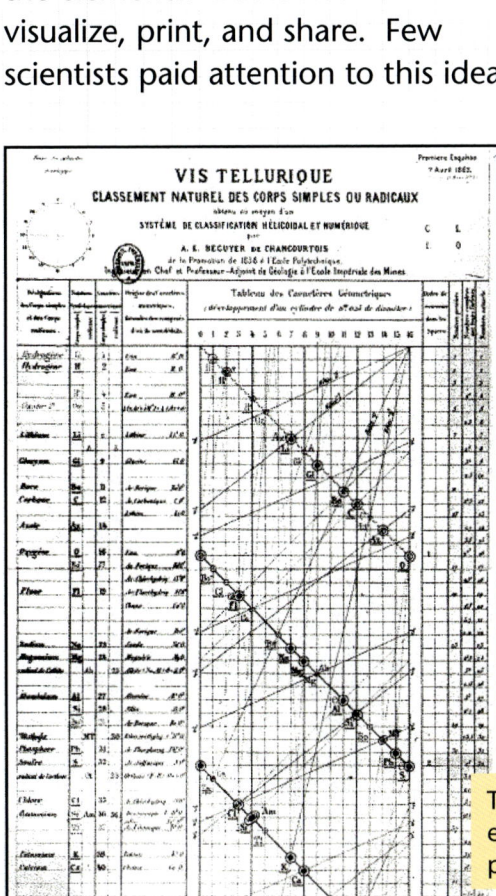

This French scientist visualized the elements as a vertical spiral and plotted them on a graph.

Dmitri Mendeleev

In the 1860s, Dmitri Mendeleev was a Russian chemistry student. At that time, 60 elements were known. Mendeleev worked with all of them. He studied their properties. He spent time thinking about how elements reacted with one another. Understanding those relationships was important to him. His work revealed that **atomic weights** are key components of elements. He discovered that the number of protons in an atom's nucleus mattered. At first, many scientists thought this was just a quirk of nature. But with time, they realized that Mendeleev had discovered something important.

FUN FACT

Much of chemistry was still a mystery when Mendeleev created his periodic table. So, he left a few gaps in his chart. These were placeholders for elements that he thought might be discovered some day. His arrangement of the elements did not attract a lot of attention at first. But when new elements were found between 1875 and 1886, they fit right into his table. Chemists began to take notice!

Gallium was one of the new elements that fit into Mendeleev's table.

The idea of a periodic table came to Mendeleev in a dream. He created the first version in 1869. At least six other scientists published similar charts around the same time, but Mendeleev was the first. His straightforward chart was easy for people to read and print. His idea caught on more easily than the Telluric Screw.

Mendeleev first published his table in a chemistry textbook. He knew it wasn't complete, but he needed the money offered by the publisher. In 1871, he revised his table and repositioned elements. The table didn't simply capture his understanding of elements. It also predicted what elements would be discovered many years later.

the first version of the periodic table

Further Discoveries

In the 1890s, **noble gases** were discovered. These elements took longer than others to be discovered because they rarely react with other elements. Some of them are odorless, colorless, and tasteless. This made them hard to find! But it became clear that noble gases played an important role in chemistry. So, a new column for these gases was easily added to Mendeleev's table.

Even more discoveries were made in the early 1900s. In 1905, physicist Albert Einstein proved that atoms exist. His work helped chemists better understand why the periodic table looked the way it did. And in 1924, Henry D. Hubbard added more details to the table. Each element was listed with a symbol. Some symbols are easy to understand. For instance, *He* is short for helium. But *Ag* is silver because silver was originally called *argentum*. That's Latin for "shiny, gray stuff." At this time, the **atomic numbers**, the weights, and other data about the elements were also included in the table.

The 1950s saw even more changes to the periodic table. Chemists moved some elements to a separate area at the bottom of the chart. This made the chart easier to read. Soon, the charts were commonly seen in chemistry labs and high schools. In fact, this version of the table is used most often today.

2
He
Helium
4.002

10
Ne
Neon
20.179

18
Ar
Argon
32.06

36
Kr
Krypton
83.798

54
Xe
Xenon
131.293

86
Rn
Radon
222

118
Og
Oganesson
294

noble gases

The Art of Science

Science is full of numbers and complex ideas that can be difficult to digest. In the 1980s, a professor named Edward Tufte thought about this issue. He came up with ideas for how to present data. In the end, he wrote a book about how to elegantly visualize data. Scientists and designers in many fields continue to use the ideas in his beautiful book.

Henry D. Hubbard

Understanding Atomic Numbers

Scientists often talk about light and heavy elements. The words *light* and *heavy* refer to an element's atomic number. That's how many protons an atom's nucleus has. For example, uranium has an atomic number of 92. It's the heaviest element that occurs naturally on Earth.

Physicist Richard Feynman calculated that no element can have an atomic number higher than 137. Past that point, electrons in the nucleus would need to move faster than the speed of light. Moving more quickly than that is impossible. Later calculations put the limit at around 173. If the number were any higher, atoms would behave in ways that feel more "sci-fi" than scientific.

Richard Feynman

You don't need complex math to understand atomic numbers, though. The more protons in a nucleus, the more positively charged the atom is. The more positively charged it is, the more the protons repel one another. This makes for a very unstable atom. And it doesn't take long before those protons break apart! They split apart and don't hold their shape.

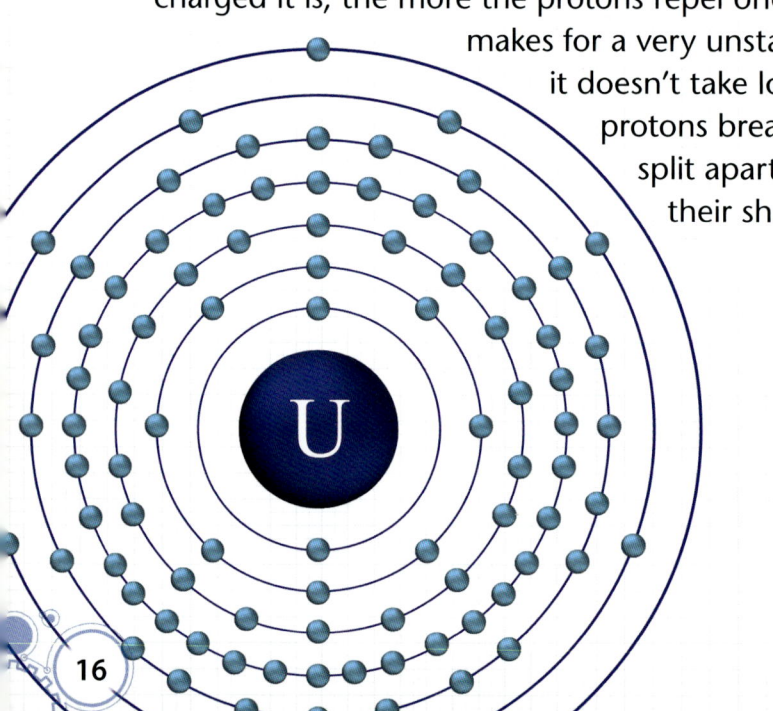

New Discoveries?

Scientists have discovered new elements thanks to special laboratories and unique tools. But these discoveries are very rare. It is often difficult to detect new elements because they are unstable. Scientists think that one promising place to look for new elements may be neutron stars. These are extremely dense stars that form in the universe. When they collide with each other, the explosion can create new elements.

neutron star

ENGINEERING

Atom Smasher

One of the tools scientists use to study atoms and particles is the Large Hadron Collider. This is the world's largest particle accelerator. It's a huge ring of strong magnets and cables. It runs underground. It has a circumference of 17 miles (27 kilometers)! Inside it, electricity sends particles flying in opposite directions at high speeds. Scientists study what happens when they collide. They have even found new particles!

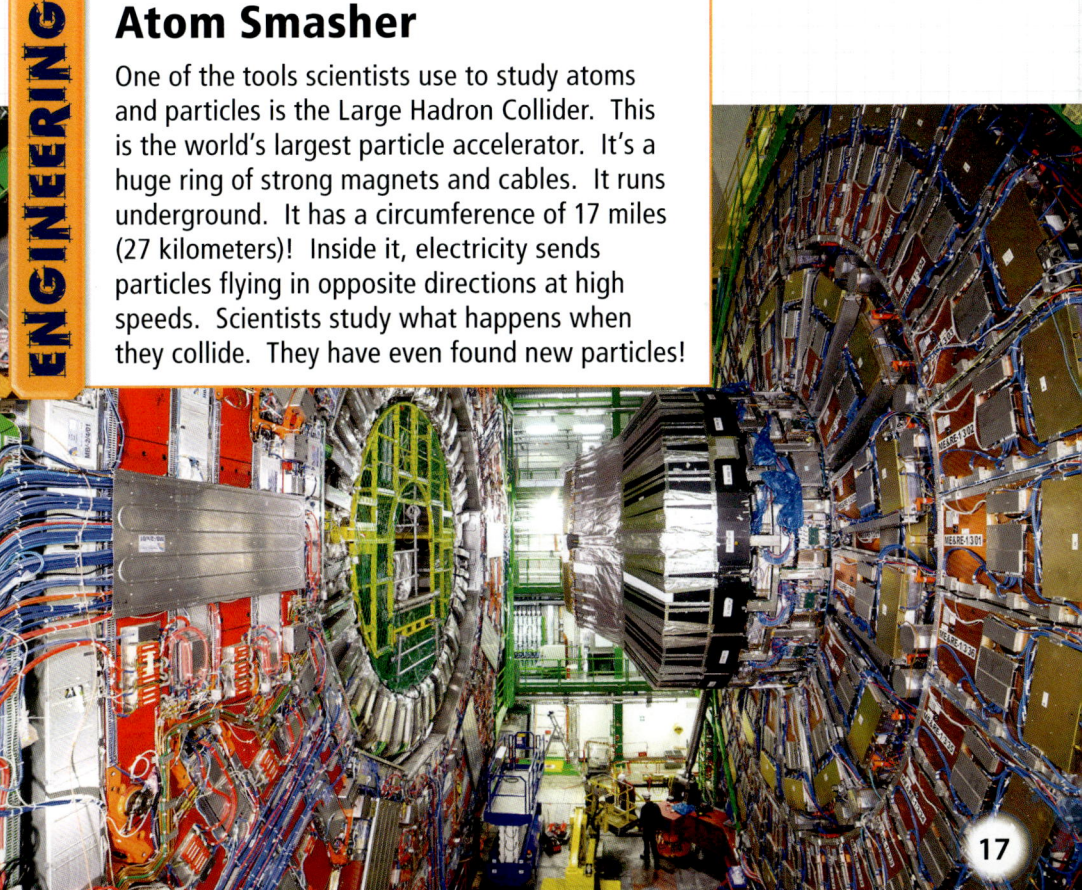

Dissecting the Periodic Table

At its core, the periodic table is a way of organizing information. The table shows the relationship between the elements. Elements in the same column are known as groups or families. They share similar properties. This means they behave in similar ways. And, the properties of each element are related to the atomic number. The periodic table reflects all this information in one place.

Reading Each Box

At the top of each box is the atomic number. Elements are listed in order of their atomic numbers. Below the atomic number is each element's symbol. Then, the element's name is spelled out.

The average atomic weight is also given. The atomic number and atomic weight might sound similar. But they refer to different properties. The atomic number tells us the number of protons in an atom's nucleus. The atomic weight tells us the average amount of matter in an atom. The matter refers to protons, neutrons, and electrons. Electrons are very light and weigh almost zero. So, protons and neutrons factor more into atomic weight than electrons.

Still, the way electrons are configured in an atom is important. This is what unites the elements in each section of the periodic table. And each entry on the table describes how the electrons are positioned. This table is an elegant way to present so much data!

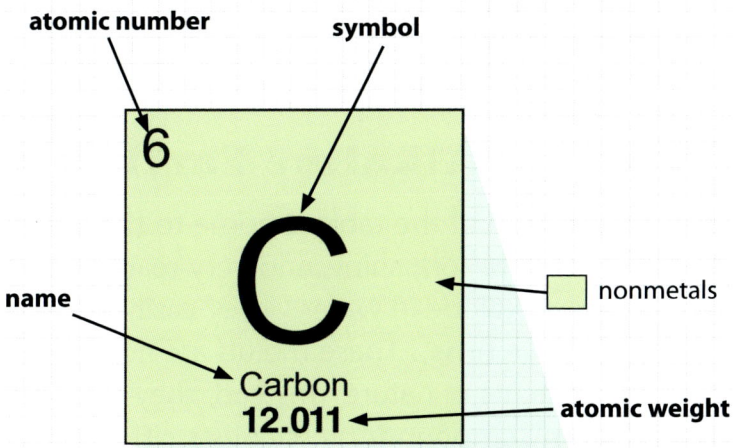

atomic number

symbol

6

C

name

Carbon
12.011

atomic weight

nonmetals

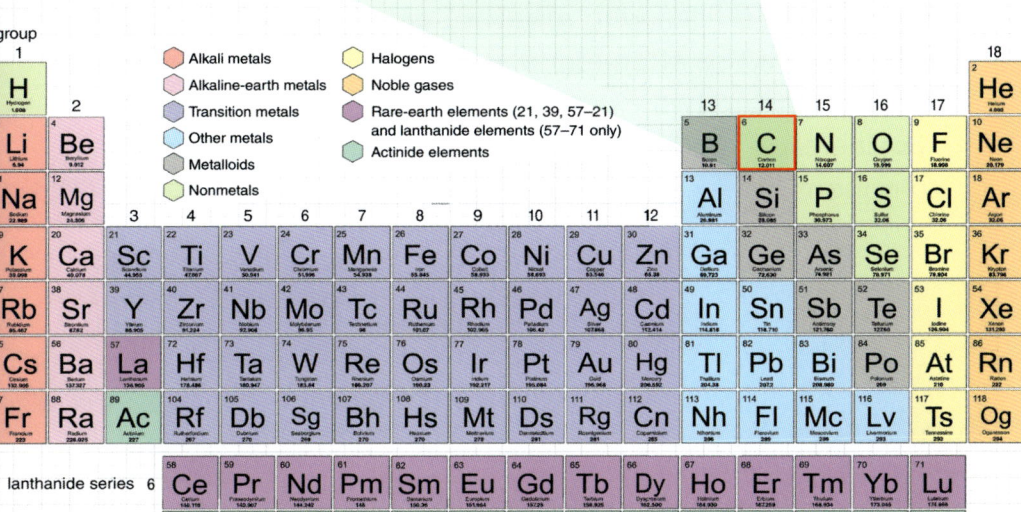

group
1

Alkali metals
Alkaline-earth metals
Transition metals
Other metals
Metalloids
Nonmetals

Halogens
Noble gases
Rare-earth elements (21, 39, 57–21)
and lanthanide elements (57–71 only)
Actinide elements

18

1	2	3	4	5	6	7	8	9	10	11	12	13	14	15	16	17	18
H																	He
Li	Be											B	C	N	O	F	Ne
Na	Mg											Al	Si	P	S	Cl	Ar
K	Ca	Sc	Ti	V	Cr	Mn	Fe	Co	Ni	Cu	Zn	Ga	Ge	As	Se	Br	Kr
Rb	Sr	Y	Zr	Nb	Mo	Tc	Ru	Rh	Pd	Ag	Cd	In	Sn	Sb	Te	I	Xe
Cs	Ba	La	Hf	Ta	W	Re	Os	Ir	Pt	Au	Hg	Tl	Pb	Bi	Po	At	Rn
Fr	Ra	Ac	Rf	Db	Sg	Bh	Hs	Mt	Ds	Rg	Cn	Nh	Fl	Mc	Lv	Ts	Og

lanthanide series 6: Ce Pr Nd Pm Sm Eu Gd Tb Dy Ho Er Tm Yb Lu

actinide series 7: Th Pa U Np Pu Am Cm Bk Cf Es Fm Md No Lr

An Elegant Idea

Scientists and mathematicians sometimes describe ideas that are simple but important as "elegant." An elegant idea feels complete. And it has far-reaching effects. This is true for the periodic table. It is also true for some equations. Some mathematicians have even called certain equations beautiful!

$$a^2 + b^2 = c^2$$

The periodic table is organized into several groups. Each one is unique and has its own properties. Let's explore them!

Alkali and Alkaline Earth Metals

The left column of the table is home to the **alkali metals**. These are soft, shiny, and very reactive elements. They can even explode in water. They easily lose electrons and form positive **ions**. These metals are not found as individual elements in nature. Instead, they're usually extracted from compounds by scientists. The second column from the left is filled with **alkaline earth metals**. These elements are also often found as positive ions. Magnesium and calcium are two examples that are abundant in nature. Alkaline earth metals are used in everything from medicines to ribbons.

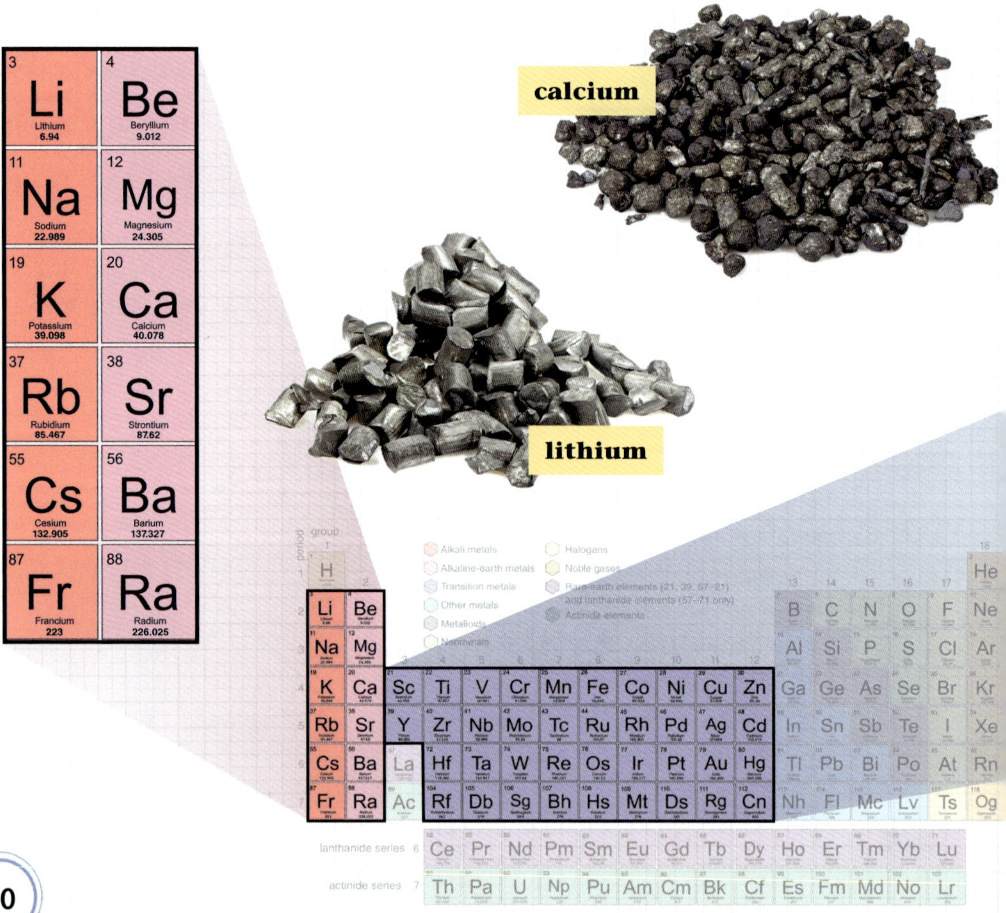

calcium

lithium

Chemistry Detectives

Did you know that there are rules about what can be included in the periodic table? One agency makes these decisions. It is called the International Union of Pure and Applied Chemistry (IUPAC). If someone says they've discovered a new element, the IUPAC investigates. They confirm the atomic weights are accurate. They determine when a new element can be added to the table. They are also responsible for the final name of the element.

Transitional Metals

The large rectangle in the middle of the table is made up of the transitional metals. Iron, nickel, and gold are found here. These elements all have electrons that can participate in chemical bonds. They are not as reactive as the previous metals. In their natural states, they are malleable, meaning they can be bent and shaped into wires and sheets of metal. These elements have high melting points and are relatively stable. Also, they conduct heat and electricity. This is another reason why they're often used in wires.

21	22	23	24	25	26	27	28	29	30
Sc	Ti	V	Cr	Mn	Fe	Co	Ni	Cu	Zn
Scandium 44.955	Titanium 47.867	Vanadium 50.941	Chromium 51.996	Manganese 54.938	Iron 55.845	Cobalt 58.933	Nickel 58.693	Copper 63.546	Zinc 65.38
39	40	41	42	43	44	45	46	47	48
Y	Zr	Nb	Mo	Tc	Ru	Rh	Pd	Ag	Cd
Yttrium 88.905	Zirconium 91.224	Niobium 92.906	Molybdenum 95.95	Technetium 98	Ruthenium 101.07	Rhodium 102.905	Palladium 106.42	Silver 107.866	Cadmium 112.414
72	73	74	75	76	77	78	79	80
Hf	Ta	W	Re	Os	Ir	Pt	Au	Hg
Hafnium 178.486	Tantalum 180.947	Tungsten 183.84	Rhenium 186.207	Osmium 190.23	Iridium 192.217	Platinum 195.084	Gold 195.966	Mercury 200.592
104	105	106	107	108	109	110	111	112
Rf	Db	Sg	Bh	Hs	Mt	Ds	Rg	Cn
Rutherfordium 267	Dubnium 270	Seaborgium 269	Bohrium 270	Hassium 270	Meitnerium 278	Darmstadtium 281	Roentgenium 281	Copernicium 285

titanium

copper

Other Metals and Nonmetals

The next four columns in the table are a mix of other metals and **nonmetals**. Common metals, such as aluminum, tin, and lead, can be found here in the blue section. These metals conduct heat and electricity easily. In the green section, nonmetals are less conductive. They tend to collapse under high voltages and heat. Nonmetals usually look dull. They may be brittle, transparent, or opaque. These nonmetals play an important role in organic chemistry. Some of them, such as carbon and oxygen, are known as the building blocks of life. These building block elements can be found in all living things. Next, **metalloids** are the elements shown in grey. They share properties with metals and nonmetals. For example, silicon is an important metalloid. It's used in computer chips.

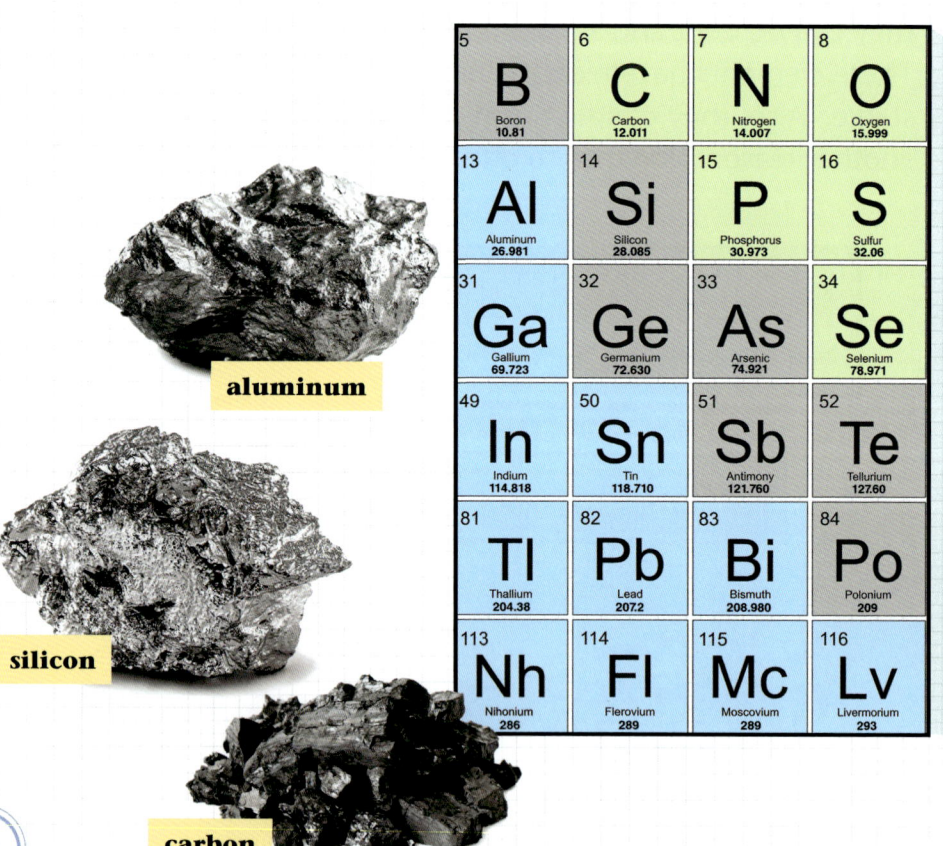

aluminum

silicon

carbon

Halogens

In the second column from the right, the table lists **halogens**. These elements tend to be negatively charged. They have more electrons than protons. They react dramatically with alkali metals and alkaline earth metals. The name *halogen* comes from the Greek words for "salt" and "to produce." All halogens can form some kind of salt. These elements are not found on their own in nature, but they are often found in combination with other elements. For example, fluorine is easily found in a combined form in Earth's crust. Sodium combines with chlorine to make sodium chloride—the table salt people eat every day.

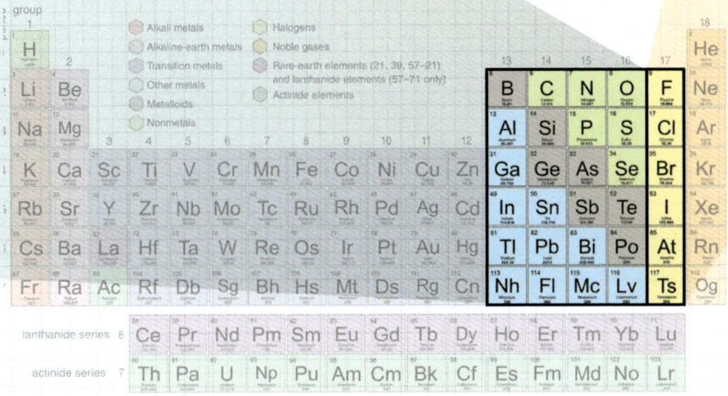

chlorine

flourine

9	
F	Fluorine 18.998

17	
Cl	Chlorine 32.06

35	
Br	Bromine 79.904

53	
I	Iodine 126.904

85	
At	Astatine 210

117	
Ts	Tennessine 293

group

1																	18
H	2											13	14	15	16	17	He
Li	Be											B	C	N	O	F	Ne
Na	Mg	3	4	5	6	7	8	9	10	11	12	Al	Si	P	S	Cl	Ar
K	Ca	Sc	Ti	V	Cr	Mn	Fe	Co	Ni	Cu	Zn	Ga	Ge	As	Se	Br	Kr
Rb	Sr	Y	Zr	Nb	Mo	Tc	Ru	Rh	Pd	Ag	Cd	In	Sn	Sb	Te	I	Xe
Cs	Ba	La	Hf	Ta	W	Re	Os	Ir	Pt	Au	Hg	Tl	Pb	Bi	Po	At	Rn
Fr	Ra	Ac	Rf	Db	Sg	Bh	Hs	Mt	Ds	Rg	Cn	Nh	Fl	Mc	Lv	Ts	Og

Alkali metals
Alkaline-earth metals
Transition metals
Other metals
Metalloids
Nonmetals
Halogens
Noble gases
Rare-earth elements (21, 39, 57–71) and lanthanide elements (57–71 only)
Actinide elements

lanthanide series 6 | Ce | Pr | Nd | Pm | Sm | Eu | Gd | Tb | Dy | Ho | Er | Tm | Yb | Lu

actinide series 7 | Th | Pa | U | Np | Pu | Am | Cm | Bk | Cf | Es | Fm | Md | No | Lr

Noble Gases

The noble gases are found in the final column of the periodic table. They tend to be very stable and nonreactive elements. They are colorless, odorless, and tasteless. Each one has a low boiling point, so it is always in gas form at room temperature. Noble gases make up a large part of the universe. Each one can be used for various purposes. For example, humans use helium to make balloons float in the air. Helium is mixed into the oxygen that deep sea divers breathe. Helium also provides stability for cutting and welding metals. Oxygen reacts to hot metal, but helium doesn't, so it's safer to use.

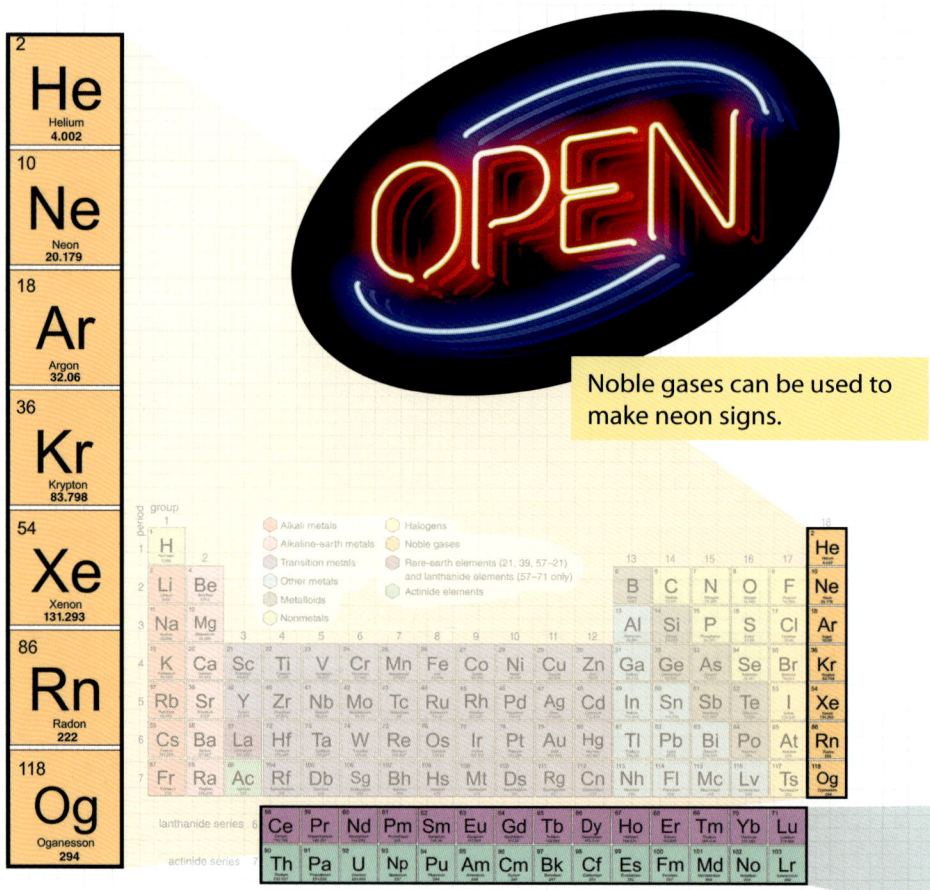

Noble gases can be used to make neon signs.

Lanthanides and Actinides

Below the main part of the periodic table are two rows of elements. Sometimes, this section is referred to as an island. There, you'll find **lanthanides** and **actinides**. These elements were mostly discovered after Mendeleev's lifetime. They are very similar to one another, so it took time to understand their unique properties.

Lanthanides are rare earth metals. They may be fluorescent, meaning they give off light, or magnetic. They are often used in new technologies. For example, smartphones and lasers depend on them. Actinides are often radioactive. They can be used to generate power. Most of them are human-made, meaning they don't occur in nature. One example of this is plutonium. This element has been used in atomic weapons.

plutonium pellet

58 Ce Cerium 140.116	59 Pr Praseodymium 140.907	60 Nd Neodymium 144.242	61 Pm Promethium 145	62 Sm Samarium 150.36	63 Eu Europium 151.964	64 Gd Gadolinium 157.25	65 Tb Terbium 158.925	66 Dy Dysprosium 162.500	67 Ho Holmium 164.930	68 Er Erbium 167.259	69 Tm Thulium 168.934	70 Yb Ytterbium 173.045	71 Lu Lutetium 174.966
90 Th Thorium 232.037	91 Pa Protactinium 231.035	92 U Uranium 231.035	93 Np Neptunium 237	94 Pu Plutonium 244	95 Am Americium 243	96 Cm Curium 247	97 Bk Berkelium 247	98 Cf Californium 251	99 Es Einsteinium 252	100 Fm Fermium 257	101 Md Mendelevium 258	102 No Nobelium 259	103 Lr Lawrencium 262

Fundamental Building Blocks

Our understanding of science is built on a chain of discoveries. Over time, chemists have learned how atoms and molecules work. Bit by bit, they've found patterns in nature and learned what those patterns mean. Their work has shaped the way humans see everything in the universe. And they found a way to capture the information they know about elements in an easy-to-follow table.

Nature doesn't always conform to systems and tables. But when humans find a way to understand a new idea, the ripple effects can be profound. Think of it this way. Imagine that the elements in the periodic table are like ingredients in your kitchen. This would mean that the periodic table is like a recipe. But it's not just any recipe—it's *the* recipe. It is the recipe for making everything.

Chemistry involves studying the structure of atoms. It helps scientists understand why electrons move from atom to atom. The periodic table shows why that sometimes happens. Most of all, the periodic table helps scientists do more than guess. It helps them make accurate predictions. It shows them what's possible. Finally, it makes the invisible visible in a beautiful, orderly way. Chemists, and all of us, would be lost without the periodic table!

STEAM CHALLENGE

Define the Problem

The periodic table has been a source of inspiration for art, accessories, and decor. A children's furniture and decor company is working on a line of science-themed items for budding scientists. They have asked you to create a mobile inspired by the periodic table. It needs to be hangable in a nursery or in a young child's room.

Constraints: You may only use the materials provided to you.

Criteria: Your mobile must include representations of at least three different elements from the periodic table. It must be able to hang and remain intact. It must be visually appealing so customers will want to buy it and babies or young children will enjoy looking at it.

Research and Brainstorm

What are some common or interesting mobile designs? What do you like and dislike about these designs? Which ideas do you think would work well for a periodic table mobile? What materials will work best to make this type of item? How could you represent different elements?

Design and Build

What are some common or interesting mobile designs? What do you like and dislike about these designs? Which ideas do you think would work well for a periodic table mobile? What materials will work best to make this type of item? How could you represent different elements?

Test and Improve

Hang your mobile and show it to others. Explain how it meets the criteria. Ask for feedback. What could you add or adjust to make it more visually pleasing? Do you want to add any moving parts? How else can you improve it? Modify your design and rebuild it as needed. Reassess how well it meets the criteria.

Reflect and Share

What about this challenge was the most difficult? What are you most proud of? What other materials would you have liked to use? What other items could you create for a nursery or a child's room that are on theme with the periodic table?

Glossary

actinides—heavy, radioactive metal elements that are often humanmade

alkali metals—soft, shiny, and very reactive elements

alkaline earth metals—elements that are abundant in nature and often have a positive charge

atomic numbers—numbers of protons in the nuclei of atoms

atomic weights—average amounts of matter in atoms

atoms—smallest parts of elements that can exist either by themselves or in combinations

chemistry—a science that deals with the composition, structure, and properties of substances and the changes that they go through

compounds—distinct substances formed by the union of two or more chemical elements in proportion by weight

electrons—negatively charged particles in the nuclei of atoms

elements—any of more than 100 fundamental substances that consist of atoms of only one kind

halogens—any of the five negatively charged elements that can form some kind of salt

ions—atoms or groups of atoms that have positive or negative charges

lanthanides—elements that may be fluorescent or magnetic; often used in new technology

metalloids—elements that share properties with metals and nonmetals

neutrons—uncharged particles in the nuclei of atoms

noble gases—colorless, odorless, and tasteless elements that rarely react with other elements and are always in gas form at room temperature

nonmetals—elements that tend to collapse under high voltages and heat

properties—specific qualities or traits belonging to individuals or things

protons—positively charged particles in the nuclei of atoms

subatomic—of, relating to, or being particles smaller than atoms

Index

CAREER ADVICE
from Smithsonian

Do you dream of studying chemistry?

Here are some tips to keep in mind for the future.

"Understanding chemistry helps us understand the world around us. Everything from salt on our food, to clouds in the sky, to volcanic eruptions, involves chemistry."

– *Benjamin Andrews*, *Geologist and Associate Curator of Rocks and Ores, National Museum of Natural History*

"The periodic table helps make sense of the building blocks that make up everything around us."

– *Gabriela Farfan*, *Research Geologist, National Museum of Natural History*